MOM'S FUN-SCHOOLING Handbook

Email:

Address:

Date:

By Sarah Janisse Brown
The Thinking Tree Publishing company, LLC

This book is designed to
INSPIRE YOU!

1. To enjoy being a mom and homemaker.

2. To enjoy being a homeschool mom.

3. To create a FUN learning environment.

 4. To care for your own needs as a woman who needs to grow in strength, wisdom, faith, understanding, compassion, creativity and kindness.

5. To spark lots of new ideas for making learning joyful for your family.

6. To help you organize your stuff so you can use what you have to the fullest.

7. To help you to be an example to your children when you "work" in this workbook.

Flip to the Back to Learn about the Author!

Flip to Fun-Schooling! Discover How to Learn Real Life Skills, Without Dull Lessons, Worksheets and Classrooms!

Underline things your children have done— that's a great start!

Circle things you want them to do. Make your own list too!

- Read Interesting Books
- Build with Legos
- Explore Nature
- Observe Animals
- Explore Wildlife
- Bake Cupcakes
- Plan a Party
- Create a Collection
- Make Your Own Book
- Travel
- Dream about the Future
- Sing Silly Songs
- Create a Scrapbook
- Look at old Photos
- Take New Pictures
- Talk to a Real Scientist
- Draw & Color Detailed Pictures
- Count Stars
- Catch Bugs
- Swim & Splash
- Invent New Ideas
- Tame a Pet
- Play Minecraft
- Watch Interesting Documentaries
- Go to the Library
- Interview Grandparents
- Build a fort
- Camp or Hike
- Science Experiments
- Enter a Contest
- Help a Person in Need
- Learn a New Skill
- Play Sim City
- Make Dinner
- Make a Birthday Card
- Try a New Recipe
- Volunteer
- Have a Yard Sale
- Write a Song

- Play Board Games
- Play Guessing Games
- Learn to Clean
- Build a Robot
- Take apart old Electronics
- Build a Computer
- Plant a Garden
- Keep a Diary
- Audition for a Play
- Film your own Reality Show
- Make a Stop Action video
- Make Animals with Clay
- Water Color
- Learn to Sew
- Collect Coins from other Countries
- Make a Treasure Map
- Organize a Race
- Go on a Scavenger Hunt
- Tie-dye old Clothing
- Join a Parade
- Participate in 4H
- Paint your room a new color
- Paint on Canvas
- Freeze Juice Popsicles
- Plan a Dream Vacation
- Build a Website
- Tour a Factory
- Go to Work with an Adult
- Melt Chocolate & Peanut Butter
- Bake Cookies
- Plant a Tree
- Pick Berries
- Identify Animal Tracks
- Make a Recipe Box
- Make a Pizza
- Make Food from Other Parts of the World
- Help Orphans
- Go on a Mission Trip
- Paint a Mural

Let's Begin..! Here are some Cute Ideas
For Creating
Fun-Schooling Baskets!

There are so many ways to make learning fun and orderly for your kids, but STOP! You need to take care of yourself before you focus on Homeschooling. The first basket you make is JUST for YOU!

Make a Mom-Time Basket

Everything you need for Mom-Time should be in a pretty basket.

Spend a little time everyday with your basket of good things!

Fill Your Basket With Good Things!

You have so many wonderful books waiting on the shelf!
Put some inspirational books into your basket. Draw the covers of
those books here.

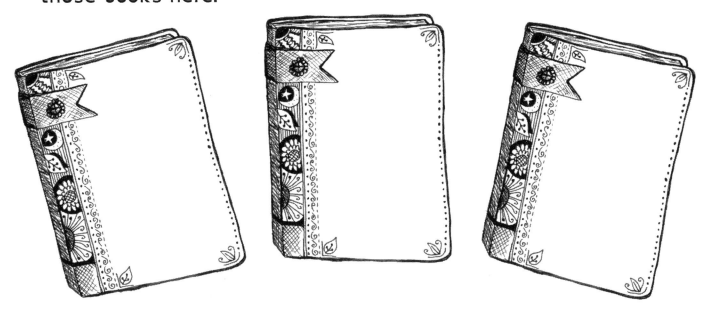

What to put in your Basket:

Your Favorite Books, A Smooth Black Pen, Colored Pencils & Gel Pens, Coffee Cup,
Candles, Matches, This Journal, Sugar, Coffee, Tea & Chocolate...

Make FUN-Schooling Baskets! Your Kids Will LOVE THEM!

We made FUN-Schooling Books and Journals to go along with all the baskets in this Idea Book!

You can Find them all on Amazon, just Look For My Name: Sarah Janisse Brown

There are over 250 FUN-Schooling Books something for every age, Stage and interest! From age 3 to adult!

THINK OF THINGS THAT YOU WOULD LIKE TO INSPIRE YOUR CHILDREN TO LEARN ABOUT.

Collect books, games and supplies that will spark their curiosity about each topic. Create Themed Fun-Schooling Baskets to use during learning time. If you have several children they can take turns using the learning baskets, or work as a team! Use the things you have at home already.

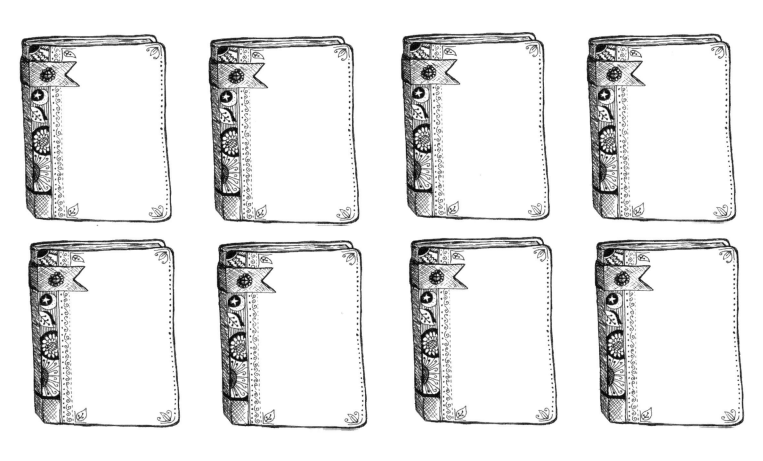

Think About All the People who are important to you. How can you bless them this week?

HOW PEOPLE
LEARN

THE 5 KEYS
1. SPARK
2. QUEST
3. Discovery
4. SHARING
5. CREATING

FUN-SCHOOLING Ideas!

_____

_____

_____

_____

_____

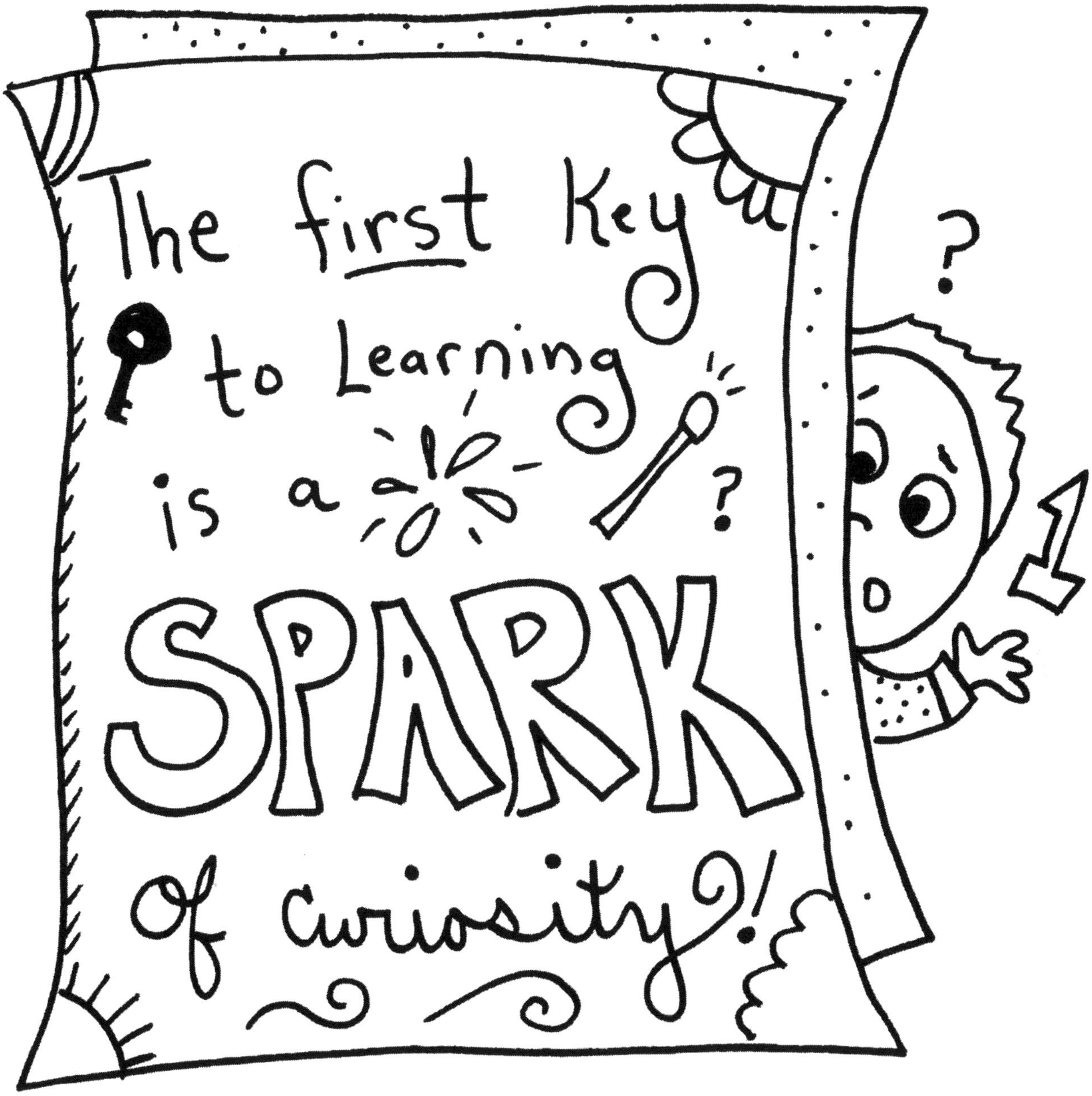
The first Key
to Learning
is a
SPARK
of curiosity!

FUN-SCHOOLING Ideas!

_____
_____
_____
_____
_____

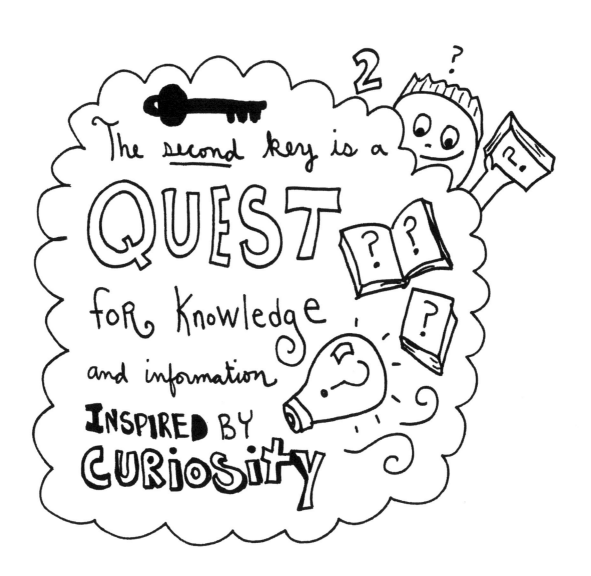

The second key is a

QUEST

for Knowledge

and information

INSPIRED BY

CURIOSITY

2

FUN-SCHOOLING IdeaS!

_____

_____

_____

_____

_____

FUN-SCHOOLING Ideas!

FUN-SCHOOLING Ideas!

_____

_____

_____

_____

_____

FREEDOM Liberty and LACK Create the Ideal ENVIORNMENT FOR INVENTION

Read Sarah's Book "How To Homeschool"
for More about the Five Keys to Learning!

Finish the Doodle

Add your own thoughts, ideas and art...

Rose Kolterman

We flipped, flopped, and fell into fun-schooling because we (the parents) are fun loving and our house is full of fun loving kids ages 2 to 10. I want my kids to love and enjoy learning; to discover their gifts, talents and interests and to have the freedom and time to pursue those things. The Thinking Tree books give just enough structure and inspiration to get us moving down the drive of delight directed developmental play and learning.

Creative Journaling

_____
_____
_____
_____
_____
_____
_____
_____
_____
_____
_____
_____
_____
_____
_____
_____
_____
_____

Reading Time

Take a book from your basket,
and make yourself a cup of tea,
Track down the secret chocolate
And take some time to read.

Live for
the Things
that
Matter Most.

What is on Your Mind?

Draw or write about all the things that have
been on your mind lately.
Writing down your thoughts can help you to
clear your mind and focus on your true priorities.

My Children Want to Learn:

Things to Plan & Organize:

Goals For this Week:

FUN-SCHOOLING Ideas!

_____
_____
_____
_____
_____
_____

Color Together

Color Together

Learn a New Skill

Have a lesson, watch a tutorial or practice your skill.

I am learning how to:

DATE:

TIME:

Goals:

Notes:

Notes:

Reading Time

Take a book from your basket,
and make yourself a cup of tea,
Track down the secret chocolate
And take some time to read.

Color Together!

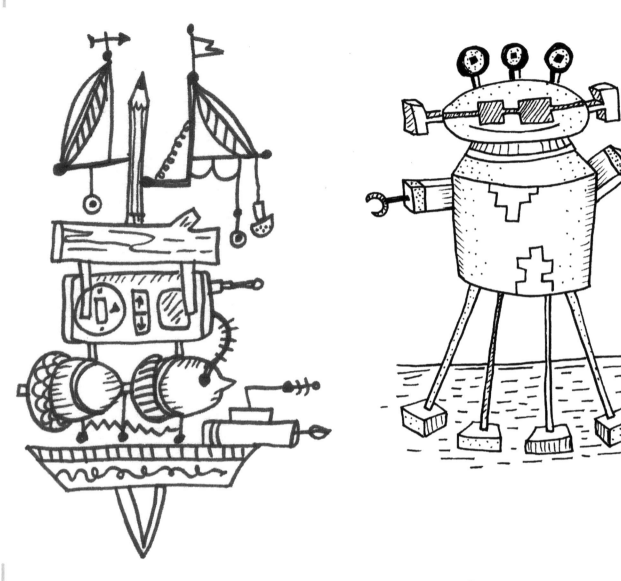

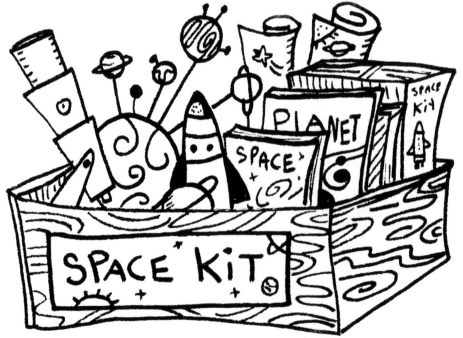

SPACE KIT

FUN Things to Do Together

FUN-SCHOOLING Ideas!

_____

_____

_____

_____

_____

_____

Creative Journaling

_____
_____
_____
_____
_____
_____
_____
_____
_____
_____
_____
_____
_____
_____
_____
_____
_____
_____
_____
_____
_____

Finish the Doodle

Add your own thoughts, ideas and art...

Martina Chymist Bump

I have decided to flip to fun-schooling because after using the traditional method of homeschooling and seeing my children struggle so much I had to do something to help them . I decided to take a different approach. I made sure that games, toys or even most of the T.V. programs they watched had an educational benefit to them. I wanted to make sure that everything they did helped them learn something.

Creative Journaling

_____

_____

_____

_____

_____

_____

_____

_____

_____

_____

_____

_____

_____

_____

_____

_____

_____

_____

_____

FUN-SCHOOLING Ideas!

_____
_____
_____
_____
_____

Thinking Time

This is where you write down your ideas, goals, and plans - with a thankful heart!

Ideas

Goals

I Am Thankful For...

Checklist

A Hope, A Prayer or A Memory

It could be a poem, a story from today

It could be a song you sing

Or a prayer you need to pray

Illustrated TO-DO List

Share This Page
With Someone You Love

GoaLS For My HoMe:

MY favorite Books!

Reading Time

Take a book from your basket,
and make yourself a cup of tea,
Track down the secret chocolate
And take some time to read.

Finish the Doodle

Add your own thoughts, ideas and art...

There are times when you must say no to something good, for the sake of Something Better.

Jennifer Fraunfelder We Flipped to Fun-Schooling because our girls were beginning to get bored with their regular curriculum we were using and I tried to find anything and everything I could to bust their boredom. Fun-Schooling has allowed my girls to study what they want to study and on their terms. They are so much more prouder of their school work and put more efforts in to their work as well. And they enjoy going to the library and picking out their books that they want to utilize with their journals. From the Winter Journal, we went on to purchase the Multiplication Games book. Since purchasing the Multiplication Games Journal, my girls are working much faster at multiplying and are loving math. I no longer hear groans and moans of discontent when it's time to do math. And it has also helped them with their division as well. Fun Schooling has really changed our homeschooling for the better.

Creative Journaling

_____
_____
_____
_____
_____
_____
_____
_____
_____
_____
_____
_____
_____
_____
_____
_____
_____
_____
_____
_____

My Children Want to Learn:

Things to Plan & Organize:

Goals For this Week:

FUN-SCHOOLING IDeaS!

GAMES + puzzles

MOM'S WORD STUDY
COMPASSION

What is Compassion?

Clue: Look in the Bible

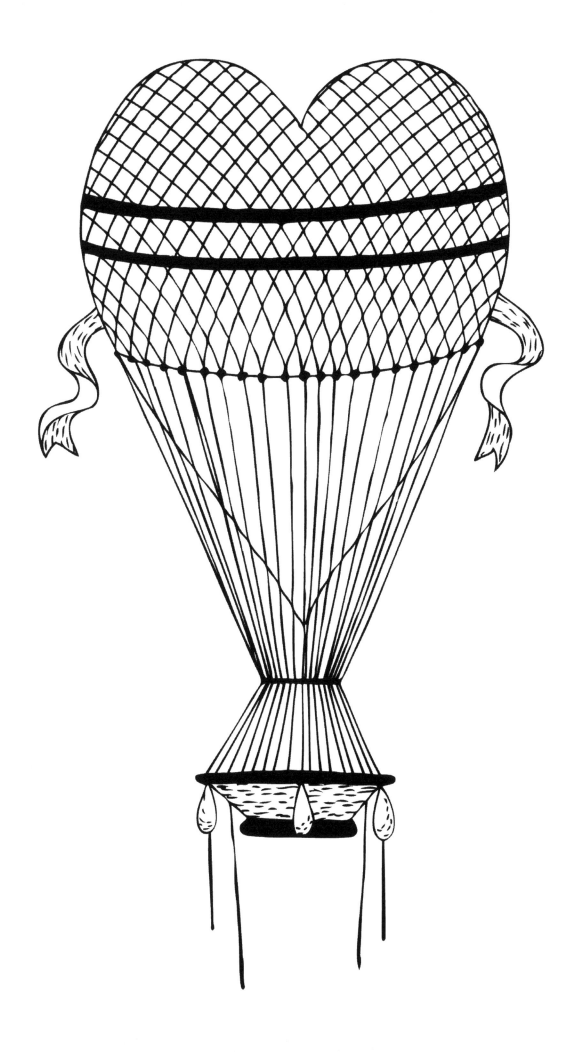

Never Forget...

Finish the Doodle

Add your own thoughts, ideas and art...

Ronda Wilson Hinzman

I have always been drawn to the Fun Schooling method of education, but have always felt in-adequate and at a loss to provide the documentation needed for our state's required annual assessment. After graduating 3 students who followed a traditional workbook curriculum I found The Thinking Tree Journals! These books have given me the confidence to allow my 2 remaining high school students to flip to delight directed learning. The journals, written to the student, will guide them in selecting topics, books, videos and more that will lead them into studying their interests.

Creative Journaling

_____

_____

_____

_____

_____

_____

_____

_____

_____

_____

_____

_____

_____

_____

_____

_____

_____

_____

_____

_____

_____

I am thankful for...

My Children Want to Learn:

Things to Plan & Organize:

Goals For this Week:

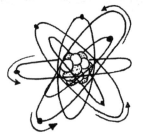

THINKING TiME

This is where you write down your ideas, goals, and plans - with a thankful heart!

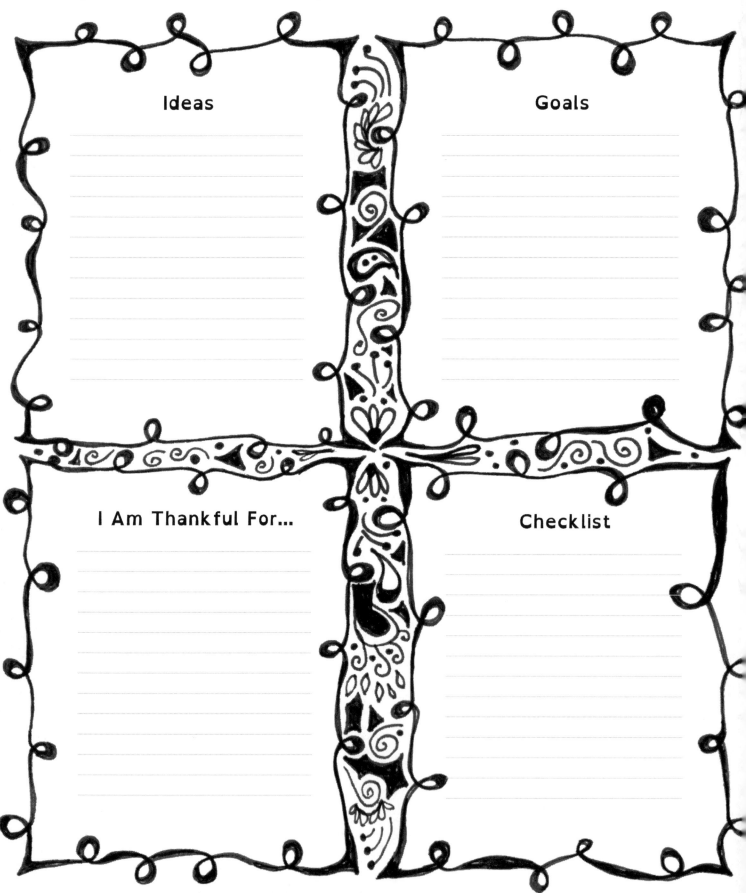

Ideas

Goals

I Am Thankful For...

Checklist

DrawiNg TiMe

Drawing Time

Finish the Doodle

Add your own thoughts, ideas and art...

Candice Forte

Since we flipped to fun-schooling he is LEARNING instead of just filling out a ton of worksheets with tear stains on them. When Daddy comes home from work he can tell him what he learned. He even does oral retelling of stories. His curriculum wanted him to retell the historical things we were reading about but that was not something that was easy. We still read all of that as part of our fun-school but I am reading him Grimm's fairy tales now and having him retell. He can do it! And I thought he was weak in that area. The freedom of fun-schooling has given us a broader education instead of the more narrow one we had been living.

Creative Journaling

_____
_____
_____
_____
_____
_____
_____
_____
_____
_____
_____
_____
_____
_____
_____
_____
_____
_____
_____
_____
_____

Hopes & Prayers

Listening Time

Listen to an audio book or classical music or ask someone to read a story to you while you color and draw on the next page.

What are you listening to?

_____

Finish the Doodle

Add your own thoughts, ideas and art...

Michelle McColl

We flipped to fun-schooling for many reasons. My health over the past few years has been quite an issue causing many days without school as I just didn't have the energy, and I think overall we were just all weary and overwhelmed with always feeling we had to catch up. I also have a son with learning issues who didn't want to read because it was too hard. Finding books he is interested has been the key. He is loving Thinking Tree Journals and Dyslexia Games. My 12 year old daughter, is loving the Journals as well., she wakes up early to work in her Homeschooling Journal and has asked to use her Journal on the weekends The enthusiasm they both have is marvelous. I love having a Mum journal. These simply are an amazing way to give your children independence in their learning but with a little structure.

Creative Journaling

_____
_____
_____
_____
_____
_____
_____
_____
_____
_____
_____
_____
_____
_____
_____
_____
_____
_____

Quotes & Verses to Remember

My Children Want to Learn:

_____

_____

_____

_____

Things to Plan & Organize:

_____

_____

_____

_____

Goals For this Week:

_____

_____

_____

FUN-SChOOLiNG IdeaS!

_____

_____

_____

_____

_____

WHat iS oN YoUr MiND?

Draw or Write about all the things that have
been on your mind lately.
Writing down your thoughts can help you to
clear your mind and focus on your true priorities.

Finish the Doodle

Add your own thoughts, ideas and art...

Shalie Gilson

I have been struggling to find peace and balance in my homeschooling. I have lots of curriculum, wonderful tools for learning, but nothing that has found the right fit. We either end up getting bored or feeling confined and our effort peters out. I was combining and splicing curriculum and spending more time on the preparation than on the teaching. We were burned out, stressed out, we had lost our love of learning and we needed desperately to rekindle that desire. When I stumbled upon Sarah's books I knew that I had found the perfect fit! We had found the perfect balance of creativity and learning. There was finally excitement about learning in our home again!

Creative Journaling

_____
_____
_____
_____
_____
_____
_____
_____
_____
_____
_____
_____
_____
_____
_____
_____
_____
_____
_____

MOM'S WORD STUDY
WISDOM

What is Wisdom?

Reading Time

Take a book from your basket,
and make yourself a cup of tea,
Track down the secret chocolate
And take some time to read.

Learn a New Skill

Have a lesson, watch a tutorial or practice your skill.

I am learning how to:

DATE:

TIME:

Goals:

Notes:

Notes:

My Children Want to Learn:

_____

_____

_____

_____

_____

Things to Plan & Organize:

_____

_____

_____

_____

_____

Goals For this Week:

_____

_____

_____

_____

Finish the Doodle

Add your own thoughts, ideas and art...

Michelle Taylor Urdak

When I began my homeschool journey, my one desire was for my children to love learning. That they would follow their curiosity to the furthest point possible. Through the first year, I bought into the lie that I needed a boxed curriculum to provide my children with the best possible education. I pushed and fought trying to fit my children into the modeled hole that was put before us. Sarah's book, "Life, Love, and Dyslexia," reminded me of why I began this journey to begin with.

I wasn't sure that fun-schooling would work for us at first, because my children are so young. It didn't take long for their natural curiosity to take over. One day I watched as a small microscope opened up my 7-year-old's mind to science, cooking taught my 3-year-old to count, and coloring helped my 5-year-old with color recognition and mine motor skills that we had been battling. That day, when everything clicked, was the most amazing, liberating day! I knew that they were learning to love learning! That's the day I became a believer!

Creative Journaling

_____

_____

_____

_____

_____

_____

_____

_____

_____

_____

_____

_____

_____

_____

_____

_____

_____

_____

_____

_____

FUN-SCHOOLING Ideas!

MOM'S WORD STUDY
FAITHFULNESS

What is Faithfulness?

Fun Things to Do Together

Thinking Time

This is where you write down your ideas, goals,
and plans - with a thankful heart!

Ideas

Goals

I Am Thankful For...

Checklist

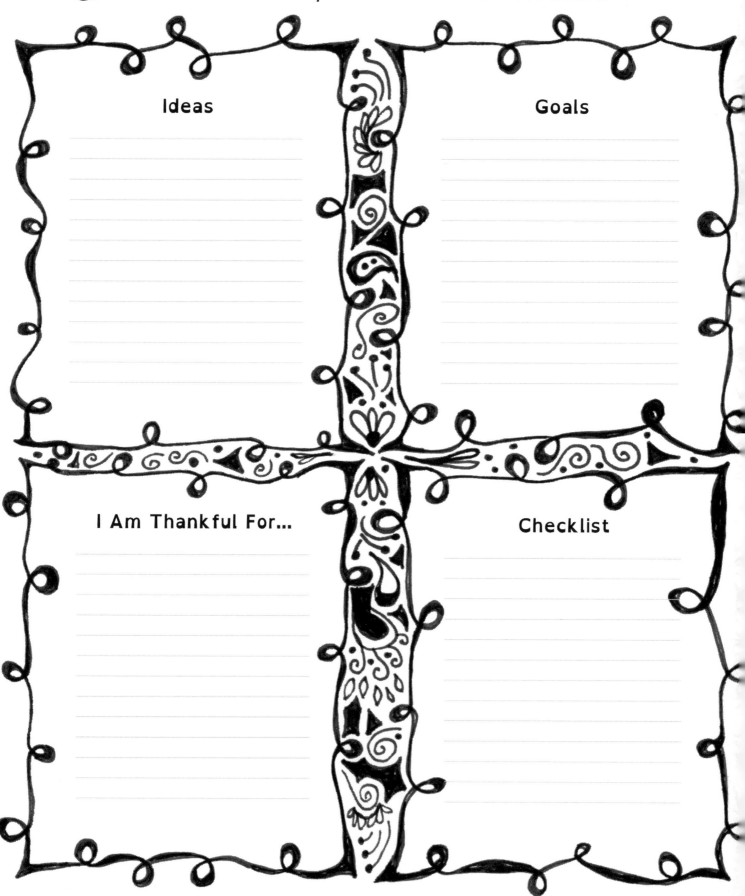

A Hope, A Prayer or A Memory

It could be a poem, a story from today

It could be a song you sing

Or a prayer you need to pray

Illustrated TO-DO List

Finish the Doodle

Add your own thoughts, ideas and art...

Julie Smith

I started out bought boxed curriculum also. We changed to Fun-School for my daughter Caitlin who is struggling with schoolwork and wanted absolutely zero to do with school of any type. I didn't know what else to do for her. She was scared to death of the special education room in public school which was offered to us to help. My boys have dyslexia, though they wanted to learn, they didn't necessary love learning. They thought it was something you did because you had to. I wanted my children to love learning. I also wanted to enjoy being their teacher. Our children respond much better to Fun-Schooling and have in return started to love learning.

Creative Journaling

_____

_____

_____

_____

_____

_____

_____

_____

_____

_____

_____

_____

_____

_____

_____

_____

_____

_____

_____

_____

Reading Time

Take a book from your basket,
and make yourself a cup of tea,
Track down the secret chocolate
And take some time to read.

MOM'S WORD STUDY
HONESTY

What is Honesty?

Clue: Look in the Bible

Never Forget...

I am thankful for...

My Children Want to Learn:

Things to Plan & Organize:

Goals For this Week:

Finish the Doodle

Add your own thoughts, ideas and art...

KelleySue Bain

"School is boring." "Grrr SCHOOL" " Mumble mumble, I Hate School" These are the comments and attitudes that had become the daily battle for this mom. Tears and frustration. Kids surrounded by great literature and learning opportunities, and a hate for learning was being embedded into their tender hearts. Flipping into Fun-School has turned our days back into mornings of peace, filled with the family gathered joyfully together studying our separate passions. Kids teaching parents at times. We started with a journal for each family member, now the boxed curriculum is back in the box and we are happily following our passions to learn and redeem every moment of this precious time together.

Creative Journaling

_____
_____
_____
_____
_____
_____
_____
_____
_____
_____
_____
_____
_____
_____
_____
_____
_____
_____
_____
_____

FUN-SCHOOLING Ideas!

_____
_____
_____
_____
_____

MOM'S WORD STUDY
GENEROSITY

What is Generosity?

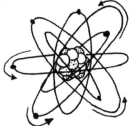

Thinking Time

This is where you write down your ideas, goals,
and plans - with a thankful heart!

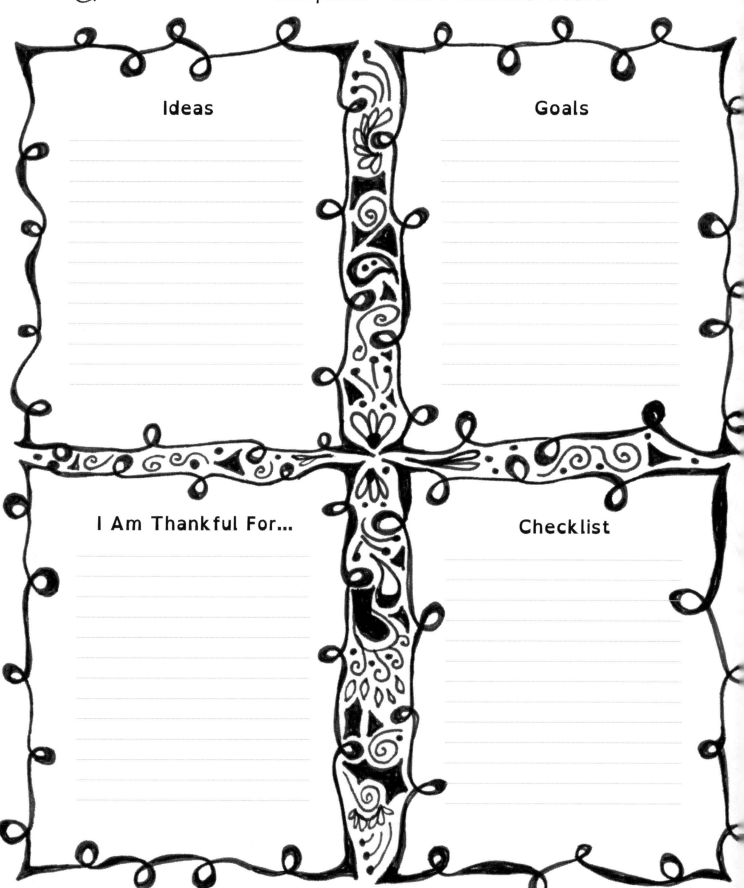

Ideas

Goals

I Am Thankful For...

Checklist

DRaWiNG TiMe

DRAWING TIME

Reading Time

Take a book from your basket,
and make yourself a cup of tea,
Track down the secret chocolate
And take some time to read.

MOM'S WORD STUDY
PATIENCE

What is Patience?

Clue: Look in the Bible

Finish the Doodle

Add your own thoughts, ideas and art...

Holley Kras

I was ready to give up homeschooling. Every day was full of stress, and anger. I was depressed and the kids were all unhappy. I had been praying on what to do. Then I stumbled on to these journals. They have changed our life. My twelve year old boy said to me yesterday, "mom, I am so happy we changed curriculum, my life has so much less stress now." I cried. This has really changed our lives.

Creative Journaling

_____

_____

_____

_____

_____

_____

_____

_____

_____

_____

_____

_____

_____

_____

_____

_____

_____

_____

_____

_____

Hopes & Prayers

Listening Time

Listen to an audio book or classical music or ask someone to read a story to you while you color and draw on the next page.

What are you listening to?

_____

Quotes & Verses to Remember

My Children Want to Learn:

_____

_____

_____

_____

_____

Things to Plan & Organize:

_____

_____

_____

_____

_____

Goals For this Week:

_____

_____

_____

_____

FUN-SCHOOLING Ideas!

_____

_____

_____

_____

_____

What will You
Do to Bless Your
Husband Today?

Finish the Doodle

Add your own thoughts, ideas and art...

Ginelle Leigh Showalter

We pulled our son from public school because bullying. We started a free, online curriculum and it was a great way to transition but I was growing concerned that my son wasn't interested in anything. He would rush through his work and then read comic books or play video games until the day was over. I wanted him to develop an interest of his own but was afraid to do it without guidance. Fun-Schooling Journals have given him a guide to explore his world. He is doing great and is exploring new books and topics. He is much more willing to do his work now. Fun-schooling also taps into the creative part of him that I didn't know we were missing.

Creative Journaling

_____

_____

_____

_____

_____

_____

_____

_____

_____

_____

_____

_____

_____

_____

_____

_____

_____

_____

_____

Reading Time

Take a book from your basket,
and make yourself a cup of tea,
Track down the secret chocolate
And take some time to read.

MOM'S WORD STUDY
SELF-DISCIPLINE

What is Self-Discipline?

Learn a New Skill

Have a lesson, watch a tutorial or practice your skill.

I am learning how to:

DATE:

TIME:

Goals:

Notes:

Notes:

Reading Time

Take a book from your basket,
and make yourself a cup of tea,
Track down the secret chocolate
And take some time to read.

Finish the Doodle
Add your own thoughts, ideas and art...

Tina Stauss

When I first started to homeschool my son I was so excited and ready. I did all my research and looked up the best curriculum that I thought he would excel at and love. Boy was I in for a surprise. Our first year did not turn out the way I had imagined nor expected. My son was unresponsive to the wonderful curriculum, in fact he didn't want to do anything. I started to worry because I knew he was smart. We had him tested and found out that he had a sensory processing disorder. He was also on the border for Dyslexia. I had to change the way I approached everything.

After a few months of more research and reading a wonderful book by Howard Gardener Frames of Mind, about the many types of intelligence. I tossed away the curriculum and amazingly found Thinking Tree Books. I love the amazing artwork, and how when you look at the books your own creativity just wants to flow. Our favorites right now are the 6 to 9 Fun Schooling Journal and Spelling Time. I am not sure what I would of done if I didn't find these great Journals. They have made the transition a little easier. I recommend the books everyday when talking to other mothers. Children are our greatest gifts, accepting them as they are and helping them as we can is our jobs as mothers. Thinking Tree has made that possible for my family.

Creative Journaling

_____

_____

_____

_____

_____

_____

_____

_____

_____

_____

_____

_____

_____

_____

_____

_____

_____

_____

_____

My Children Want to Learn:

_____
_____
_____
_____

Things to Plan & Organize:

_____
_____
_____
_____

Goals For this Week:

_____
_____
_____

FUN-SCHOOLING Ideas!

_____

_____

_____

_____

_____

Things that Need to Change in My Life

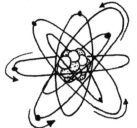

Thinking Time

This is where you write down your ideas, goals, and plans - with a thankful heart!

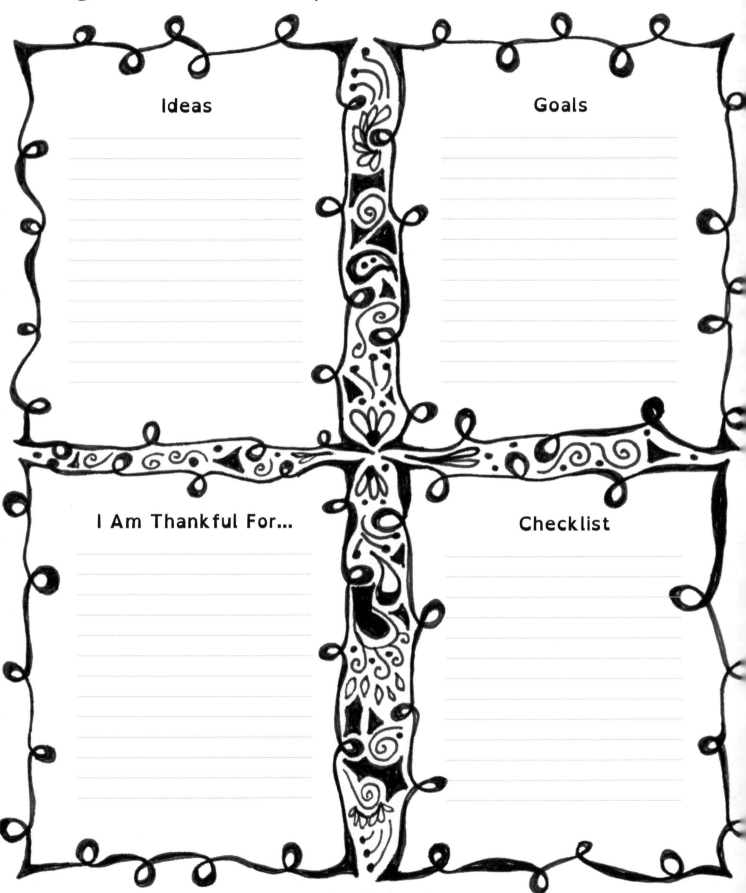

Ideas

Goals

I Am Thankful For...

Checklist

A Hope, A Prayer or A Memory

It could be a poem, a story from today

It could be a song you sing

Or a prayer you need to pray

Finish the Doodle

Add your own thoughts, ideas and art...

Lynne' Sleiman

One day my daughter hid under the table (she was 7) because she so didn't want to do her school. This was NOT what I wanted for our homeschool! I wanted her to be curious and become a life long learner! After some research into Right brain style learning I realized that I needed to find resources that fit her needs better.

She told me she wanted her school to be all about cats! I got the Kitty Doodle Curriculum, Kitty Doodle Math, Teach Yourself to Draw Cats, and all those great cat themed books from The Thinking Tree. We have spent the last few years switching every thing over to a very visual and beautiful way of learning. She no longer hides under the table, and I am enjoying our school too!

Creative Journaling

Illustrated TO-DO List

Share This Page
With Someone You Love

GOALS FOR MY HOME:

My Children Want to Learn:

Things to Plan & Organize:

Goals For this Week:

FUN-SCHOOLING Ideas!

MOM'S WORD STUDY
FORGIVENESS

What is Forgiveness?

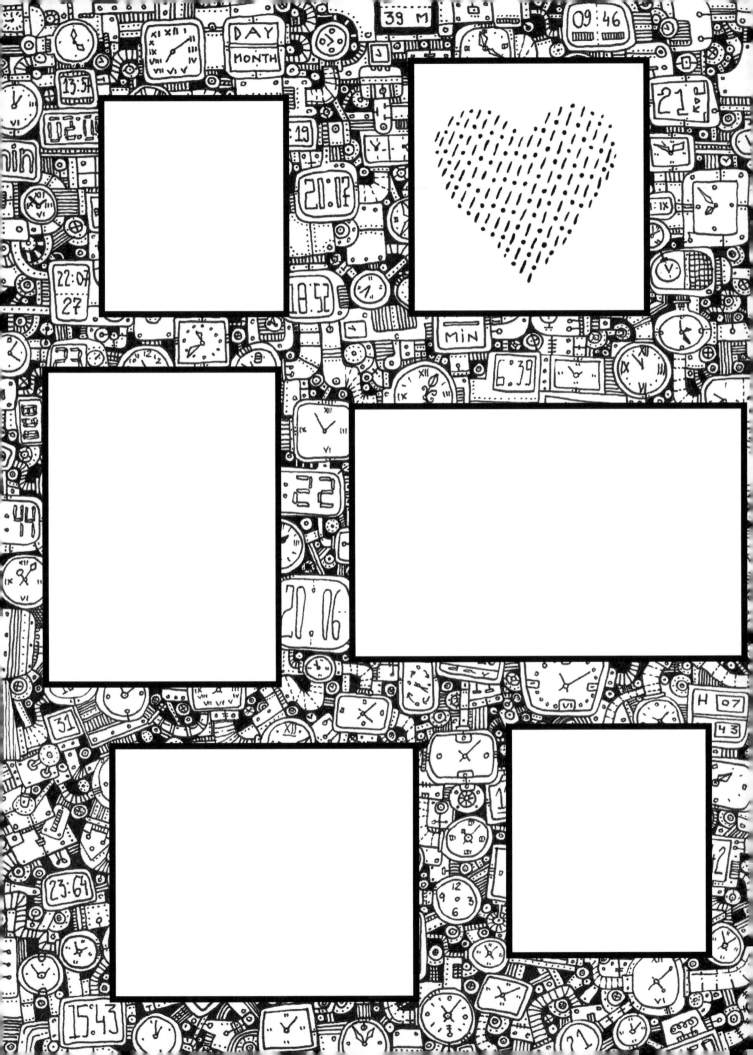

Reading Time

Take a book from your basket,
and make yourself a cup of tea,
Track down the secret chocolate
And take some time to read.

Finish the Doodle

Add your own thoughts, ideas and art...

Those who PLANT the seeds of Kindness, Will harvest the garden of Hope.

Jenn Poulin

We flipped to fun-schooling after a few attempts at "box curriculums". My son has Aspergers and ADHD and has hated school since the moment we started pre-k. He couldn't focus, he felt like he wasn't good enough since he couldn't understand, and my heart was breaking everyday. After dumping curriculum after curriculum, I knew we needed a change. I decided we would take a break, and we quit schooling all together. Then, the mom guilt set in! I felt like I wasn't doing enough and didn't have any idea where to turn. I just knew in my heart that I didn't want my son to hate school.

I was having a really emotional day when I stumbled across The Thinking Tree journals on Facebook. I was immediately hooked since my son already loved art and coloring and aspired to be an artist. I ordered right away and when we received our journals my son was very excited and I knew I made the right decision. He was happy to have something that focused on his strengths, not his weaknesses.

Creative Journaling

_____

_____

_____

_____

_____

_____

_____

_____

_____

_____

_____

_____

_____

_____

_____

_____

_____

_____

_____

Finish the Doodle

Add your own thoughts, ideas and art...

Caroline McConnell

One of the tips that Sarah had inspired me with was to emulate what you want your children to learn. ISo 've been reading more physical books in visible places and my son will now sit on the couch and read more. We have taken history books and discovered history, reading how the people lived and worked. It's this whole style of learning that just seems to expand itself and desire more learning. I realize now that I don't want my son to just parrot what is force fed to him, but I want him to be engaged by what he reads, be absorbed in the content, and most of all have a hunger for learning. What I love about the Fun-schooling concept is that it is fun, and it inspires in children the desire to learn.

Creative Journaling

_____

_____

_____

_____

_____

_____

_____

_____

_____

_____

_____

_____

_____

_____

_____

_____

_____

_____

Never Forget...

My Children Want to Learn:

Things to Plan & Organize:

Goals For this Week:

FUN-Schooling Ideas!

_____

_____

_____

_____

_____

I am thankful for...

Thinking Time

This is where you write down your ideas, goals, and plans - with a thankful heart!

Ideas

Goals

I Am Thankful For...

Checklist

My favorite Books!
I ♥ Books

Reading Time

Take a book from your basket,
and make yourself a cup of tea,
Track down the secret chocolate
And take some time to read.

Finish the Doodle
Add your own thoughts, ideas and art...

Dawn Kilgore

Every mom needs her own Coffee Time Journal and Handbook for Moms. These books can you find your joy and shalom (peace) again when life throws so much at you that you become completely overwhelmed. I will be honest, this year was the first year in my home educating journey that I almost put my children in public school against my better judgement. I was lost, I had no joy and then the Thinking Tree Journals gave us joy in learning again. We found fun-schooling when we were numb from dealing with grieving over my brother in law dying from cancer. This past year the Fun-schooling Journals and Dyslexia Games have been a God send, as I didn't know what I was doing for home-school.

Creative Journaling

_____
_____
_____
_____
_____
_____
_____
_____
_____
_____
_____
_____
_____
_____
_____
_____
_____
_____
_____
_____
_____

DRAWING TIME

DRAWiNG TiMe

Hopes & Prayers

My Children Want to Learn:

_____
_____
_____
_____
_____

Things to Plan & Organize:

_____
_____
_____
_____
_____

Goals For this Week:

_____
_____
_____

FUN-Schooling Ideas!

_____
_____
_____
_____
_____

Reading Time

Take a book from your basket,
and make yourself a cup of tea,
Track down the secret chocolate
And take some time to read.

Finish the Doodle

Add your own thoughts, ideas and art...

April MoreWills

I switched to Fun-schooling because I had been looking for engaging workbook sin black and white. My 7 year old autistic son HATES color of any kind in a book. It had lead to a general dislike of any book I suggested.

I gave him a Fun schooling for Boys and he now colors with us and there are NO tears! He gladly picks a page and participates. It is a huge improvement for our homeschool.

Creative Journaling

_____

_____

_____

_____

_____

_____

_____

_____

_____

_____

_____

_____

_____

_____

_____

_____

_____

_____

_____

Listening Time

Listen to an audio book or classical music or ask someone to read a story to you while you color and draw on the next page.

What are you listening to?

_____

Color Together

Color Together

Quotes & Verses to Remember

WHat is oN YouR MiNd?

Draw or Write about all the things that have
been on your mind lately.
Writing down your thoughts can help you to
clear your mind and focus on your true priorities.

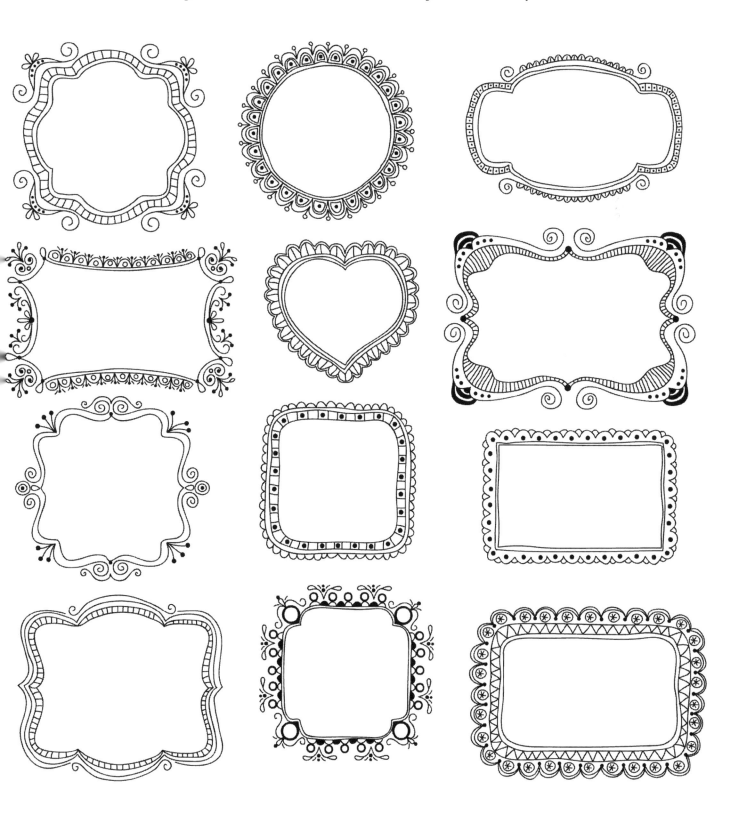

My Favorite Books!

Reading Time

Take a book from your basket,
and make yourself a cup of tea,
Track down the secret chocolate
And take some time to read.

Finish the Doodle

Add your own thoughts, ideas and art...

Erin Holdaway

I did what I had never thought possible- I pulled my son out of public school, after 8 years, and started homeschooling him. I studied curriculum and picked and chose so he would have things tailored to what I thought would be best, to how he would learn best. It took just a few months before we were both about to go crazy.

That's when I discovered The Thinking Tree and bought a journal right away. This started our journey of a more relaxed homeschool that is driven by Logan's interests. It's been much more successful. I want learning to be fun, I want him to enjoy reading, and to ask to read or write. Today he asked to make his own mini math book, so I'd say we are on the right track. My favorite Thinking Tree book so far is the Spelling Journal, followed closely by a newbie, the Littlest Math Book.

Creative Journaling

My Children Want to Learn:

_____
_____
_____
_____
_____

Things to Plan & Organize:

_____
_____
_____
_____
_____

Goals For this Week:

_____
_____
_____

FUN-SCHOOLING Ideas!

_____

_____

_____

_____

_____

What will You Do to Bless Your Husband Today?

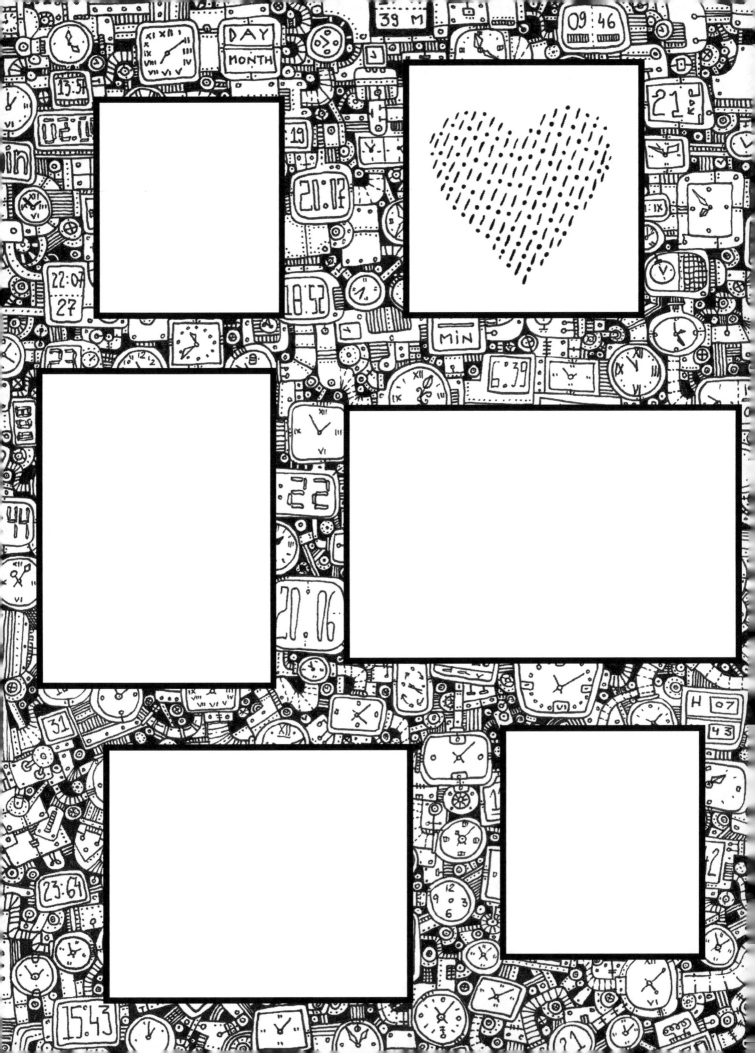

MOM'S WORD STUDY
DILIGENCE

What is Diligence?

Clue: Look in the Bible

Finish the Doodle
Add your own thoughts, ideas and art...

Bekah Gavin Brown

We flipped to fun schooling by literally diving in head first and putting all my traditional curriculum in a box (need to sell them now lol). Thanks to a friend I discovered these awesome books! My children have gone from tears to cheers with these amazing books! And why did we do it? Because school had become a constant mix of dread, tears and struggles. Now our school work is something they look forward to which means I do too!! My favorite book right now is the Moms Handbook! Its been years since I've colored and journaled. Its so nice to have some time to do something for me.

Creative Journaling

Learn a New Skill

Have a lesson, watch a tutorial or practice your skill.

I am learning how to:

DATE:

TIME:

Goals:

Notes:

Notes:

My Children Want to Learn:

_____
_____
_____
_____
_____

Things to Plan & Organize:

_____
_____
_____
_____
_____

Goals For this Week:

_____
_____
_____

FUN-SCHOOLING Ideas!

_____

_____

_____

_____

_____

Reading Time

Take a book from your basket,
and make yourself a cup of tea,
Track down the secret chocolate
And take some time to read.

FUN Things to Do Together

THINKING TIME

This is where you write down your ideas, goals,
and plans - with a thankful heart!

Ideas

Goals

I Am Thankful For...

Checklist

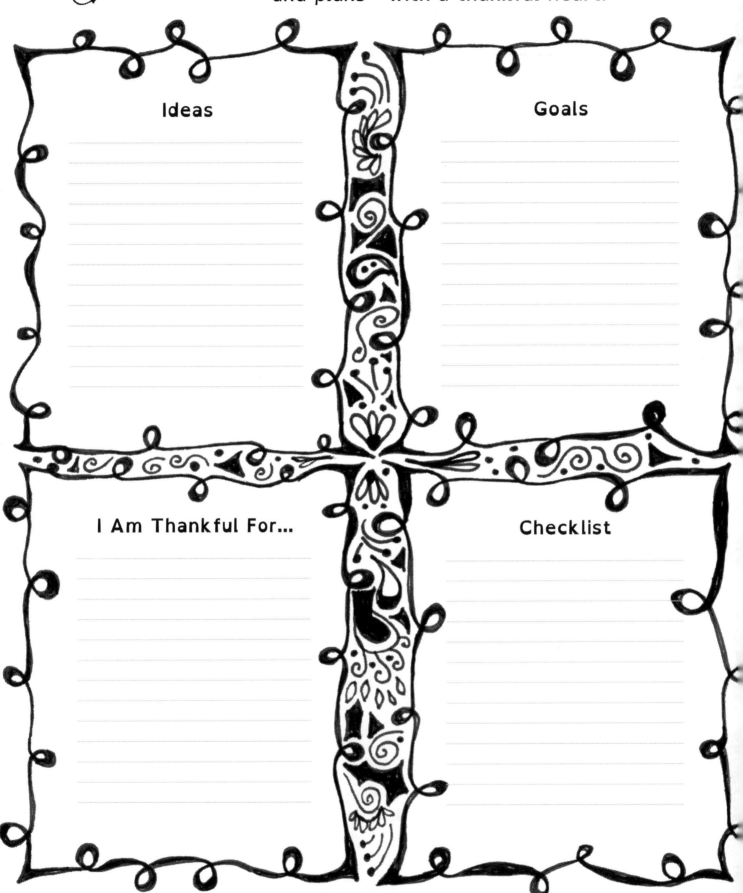

A Hope, A Prayer or A Memory

It could be a poem, a story from today

It could be a song you sing

Or a prayer you need to pray

Illustrated TO-DO List

Color Together

Finish the Doodle

Add your own thoughts, ideas and art...

Everyone Needs:
1. to UNPLUG.
2. to turn off the WiFi.
3. to go OUTSIDE.
4. to THINK.
5. to PLAY together.

Amy Pointer

At the beginning of our second year of homeschooling, I purchased a fancy $500 curriculum. It sat on the shelf for months. Nothing in our time of homeschooling was working. There was crying (on everyone's part, including mine) and fussing almost every day. I was starting to think we were going to fail at this miserably, and seeing as my son has special needs, I was VERY inclined to make it work.

Then I found Thinking Tree. I began with the 6-9 year old Fun Schooling journal, and instantly there was a change in our home. My son WANTED to do his work. He was excited about using his journal. The tears were gone. The boy who would not color was suddenly the boy who LOVED to color. Fun Schooling quickly took over our book shelf and the $500 box set made it's way to Ebay.

While we have many journals, all of which I love, my personal favorite is the Mom's Handbook. I love sitting with them and working as they work. I love having something for me that is MORE than a planner.

Thinking Tree has blessed our family with their journals, and truly changed our days.

Creative Journaling

_____
_____
_____
_____
_____
_____
_____
_____
_____
_____
_____
_____
_____
_____
_____
_____
_____
_____
_____
_____
_____
_____

Color Together

My Children Want to Learn:

Things to Plan & Organize:

Goals For this Week:

FUN-SCHOOLING IDEAS!

_____

_____

_____

_____

_____

Reading Time

Take a book from your basket,
and make yourself a cup of tea,
Track down the secret chocolate
And take some time to read.

MOM'S WORD STUDY
HUMILITY

What is Humility?

Clue: Look in the Bible

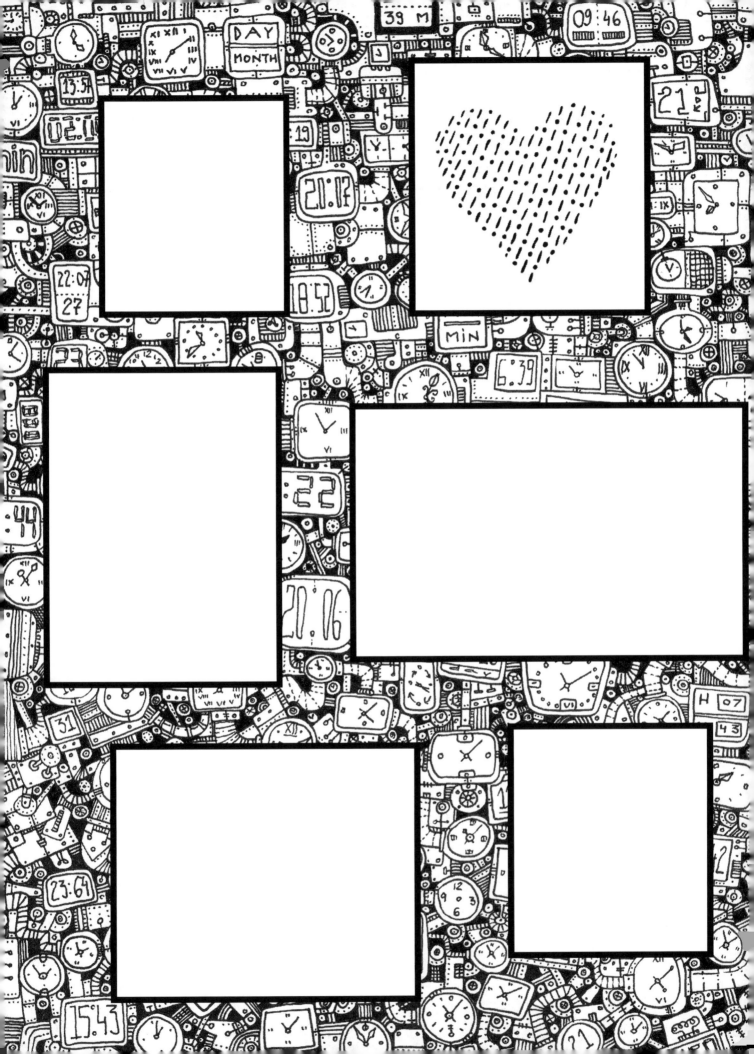

DeSigN SOMeTHiNg

It could be a dream house

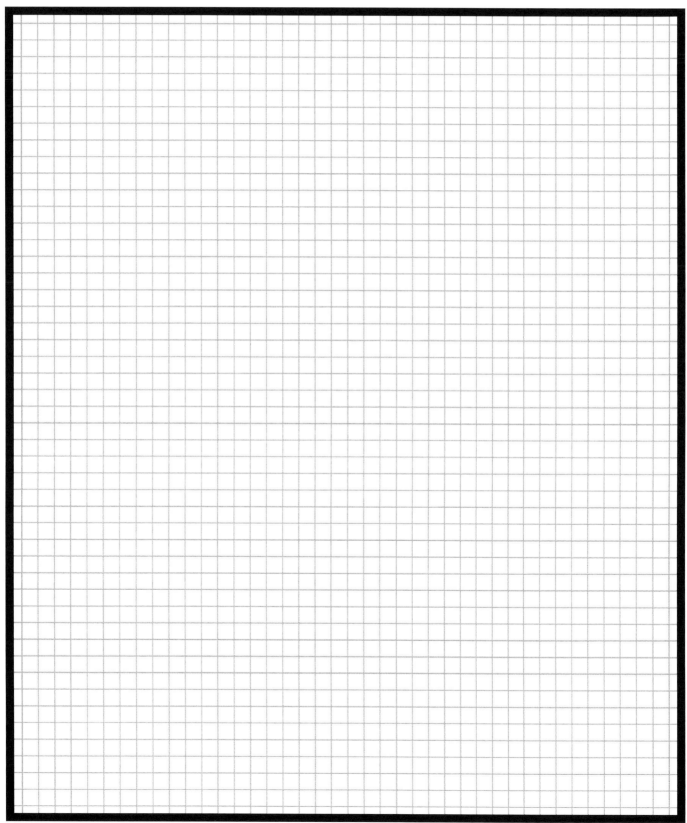

Finish the Doodle

Add your own thoughts, ideas and art...

Rosemary Morris

Our kids love the freedom of the Fun-Schooling Journals,

and they probably think they're not even doing school.

Creative Journaling

_____

_____

_____

_____

_____

_____

_____

_____

_____

_____

_____

_____

_____

_____

_____

_____

_____

_____

_____

My Children Want to Learn:

_____

_____

_____

_____

Things to Plan & Organize:

_____

_____

_____

_____

Goals For this Week:

_____

_____

_____

FUN-SCHOOLING Ideas!

Finish the Doodle

Add your own thoughts, ideas and art...

Linda Rose

We switched to fun-school simply because school had become a chore to us. The kids groaned every day as they pulled out their school books. I was sad that school had become boring and hum-drum to them. I wanted them to love to learn and also to know how to learn what they wanted to know. When I found the Thinking Tree journals, it was like a breath of fresh air! After a trip to the library, they dove into their school work like I have never seen them! They enjoy school now, and I love hearing about all the cool things they find in their books. I can see how The Thinking Tree journals gently guide them and encourage them to do their best work. Best of all they are learning and enjoying the journey. I see great potential for this type of learning and believe that for my kids the sky is the limit!

Creative Journaling

Never Forget...

Color Together

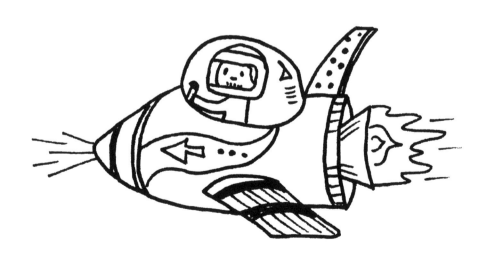

Color Together

My Children Want to Learn:

_____
_____
_____
_____
_____

Things to Plan & Organize:

_____
_____
_____
_____
_____

Goals For this Week:

_____
_____
_____

Finish the Doodle

Add your own thoughts, ideas and art...

Jamie Fuentes

Just like everything in life homeschooling has been a journey. We have tried many different curriculums and styles of learning. I still felt like something was missing. The word says "He gives us the desires of our heart" , so I just left it to Him to show me the way. We came across Dyslexia games because my second oldest was having trouble reading. We used it for awhile and then we had the chance to review Journals from The Thinking Tree. I was hooked and we dropped what we were doing and started fun schooling.

I love how you can tailor the Journals to fit your child. It is hard to do that with regular box curriculum. I have been buying books for my children when I catch them on sale. I now have plenty of books for them to read and use with their fun schooling. Before fun schooling we didn't have time to read those books because we were following the teacher's guide. Now my children are free to explore their own interest. They are learning so much.

Creative Journaling

_____

_____

_____

_____

_____

_____

_____

_____

_____

_____

_____

_____

_____

_____

_____

_____

_____

_____

_____

FUN-SCHOOLING Ideas!

_____
_____
_____
_____
_____

BABY THINGS ♥

I am thankful for...

You will never BECOME who you were MEANT TO BE →

If you just sit on your BUTT wasting TIME

What's it worth?

Finish the Doodle

Add your own thoughts, ideas and art...

Linda Beltran

I love, love, love, homeschooling my kids but at times it's tough. I felt like I was losing the joy of homeschooling. There were days that I dreamed about the big yellow school-bus driving off with my kids (I know really sad, huh). I cried out to God and cried on my husbands shoulder too saying I can't do this anymore. You'd think after homeschooling for 13+ years I'd have it all figured out. I wish but with each child so different, it's like a whole new year each every time the kids move up to the next grade. Well, God answered and I found The Thinking Tree. It was love at first site with Dyslexia Games and the journals. If you don't believe me, just ask my family.

Creative Journaling

Thinking Time

This is where you write down your ideas, goals, and plans - with a thankful heart!

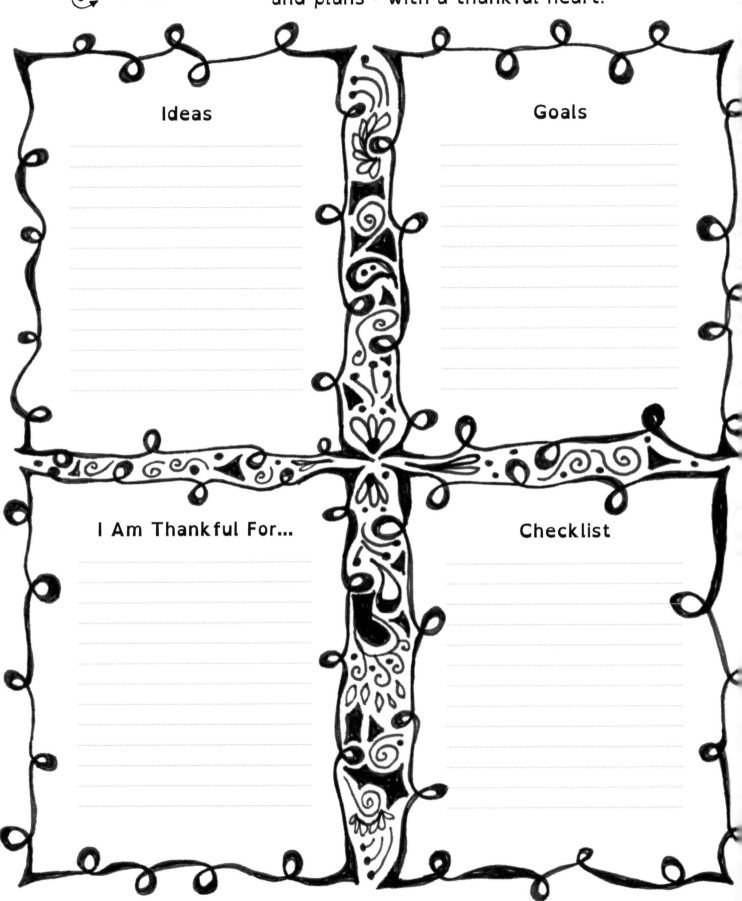

Ideas

Goals

I Am Thankful For...

Checklist

DRAWING TIME

DraWing TiMe

Hopes & Prayers

My Children Want to Learn:

_____

_____

_____

_____

_____

Things to Plan & Organize:

_____

_____

_____

_____

_____

Goals For this Week:

_____

_____

_____

FUN-SCHOOLING Ideas!

_____
_____
_____
_____
_____

Listening Time

Listen to an audio book or classical music or
ask someone to read a story to you while
you color and draw on the next page.

What are you listening to?

_____

Finish the Doodle

Add your own thoughts, ideas and art...

Jen Lakes

We flipped to fun-schooling after homeschooling for 10 years. I've tried traditional curriculum, unschooling, Charlotte Mason & finally the eclectic method. Each had their appeal for awhile, I mean who doesn't like change, right? But they each would lack some element that I couldn't put my finger on until now. Strict schedules took the joy of learning and discovery from my children. Eventually whichever method we tried whittled down to boring, repetitious & lackluster. After reading Sarah's book 'How to Homeschool' I realized it's the JOY of discovery that was missing! I had robbed my children of their joy trying to make them "finish school" before the fun could begin...ugh! Now we have fun and ENJOY school as each of us discover and learn together & independently. I have my Mom Journal that I work on while the kids work in theirs. Its brought us together & the JOY is back in our homeschool JOURNEY!

Creative Journaling

_____
_____
_____
_____
_____
_____
_____
_____
_____
_____
_____
_____
_____
_____
_____
_____
_____
_____
_____
_____

FUN-SCHOOLING PLANS FOR THE FUTURE

Thinking Tree
JOURNALS

Copyright Information

Contact Us:

The Thinking Tree LLC
617 N. Swope St. Greenfield, IN 46140. United States
317.622.8852 PHONE (Dial +1 outside of the USA) 267.712.7889 FAX
FunSchoolingBooks.com
jbrown@DyslexiaGames.com

Happy Homeschooling!

From The Browns!

Josh & Sarah

Isaac, Anna, Estera, Rachel,
Naomi, Susannah, Laura,
Joseph, Ember & Leah

Visit Sarah's Blog
WWW.StillSmiling.Net

WWW.DyslexiaGames.com

Find These and More on Amazon.com!
Just Search For Sarah Janisse Brown!

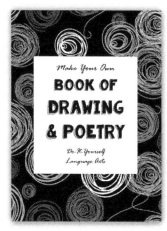

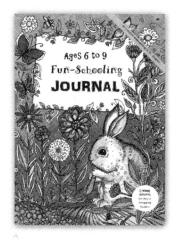

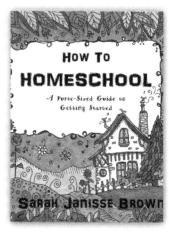

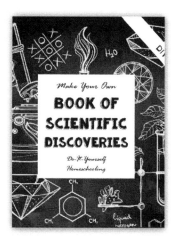

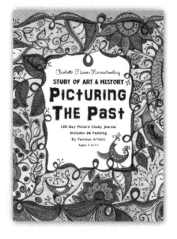

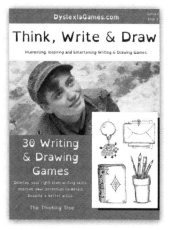

Made in the USA
San Bernardino, CA
16 June 2016